Cattitudes

Cattitudes

Victoria Roberts

VILLARD · NEW YORK · 1995

Villard Books is a registered trademark of Random House, Inc.

Library of Congress Cataloging-in-Publication Data
Roberts, Victoria
Cattitudes/ by Victoria Roberts.
p. cm.
ISBN 0-679-42361-3
1. Cats—Caricatures and cartoons. 2. American wit and humor,
Pictorial. I. Title.
NC1429.R63A4 1995
741.5'973—dc20 95-10252

Manufactured in Italy

9 8 7 6 5 4 3 2

First Edition

For Shirley A Wright

Cattitudes

Cats of
Singular
Talent

Henry & Anaïs

Gertrude & Alice

Cocteau

Frida Kahlo

Merce
—
8

Emily Dickinson & Elizabeth Bishop

Marianne Moore

Rodin

Matisse

13

Aged 5   Aged 25

Mozart

14

Andy

15

Proust

16

Cats of
the Cloth

Rasta

20

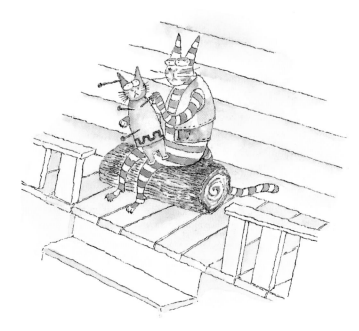

Voodoo

Shakers

Whirling Dervishes

Monks

24

Novices

Four Cardinals

26

1/2 Dozen Nuns, Barefoot

Self-Portraits

Self-portrait no. 57, Origami

Self–portrait no. 72, Topiary

Self-portrait no. 33, Catware

Self-portrait no. 14, In a Bowl of Cream

Self-portrait no. 54, T-shirt

Self-portraits nos. 74 through 642, Booth

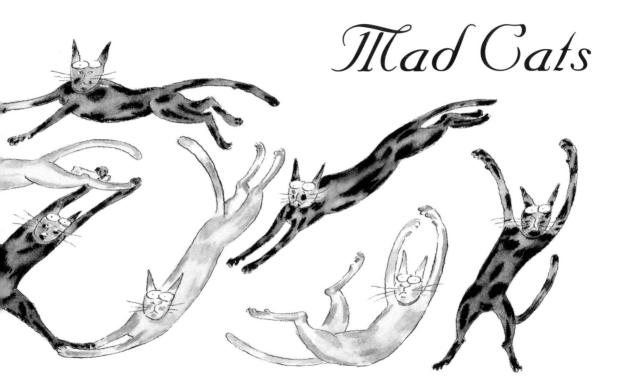

Mad Cats

January

February

March

April

May

June

July

August

Analysis

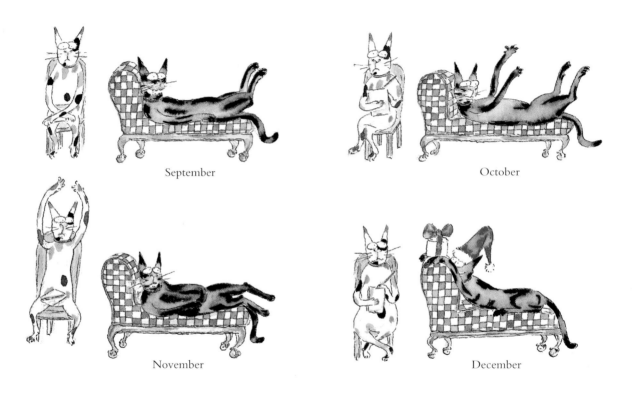

September

October

November

December

Transference

Art Therapy

42

Prozac

43

Group

45

Masters & Johnson

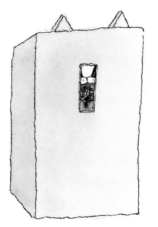

Orgone Energy Accumulator

Bad Cats

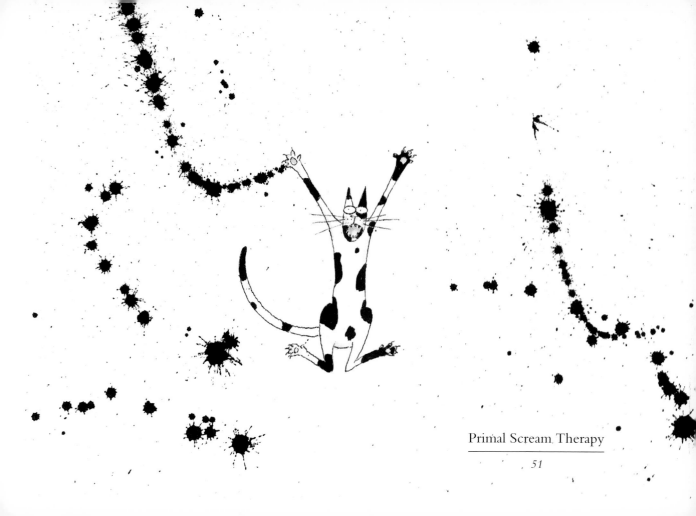

Primal Scream Therapy

Small Pleasures

Small Pleasure no. 18, Falconry

Small Pleasure no. 1, Lox

Small Pleasure no. 37, Siamese Sewing Circle

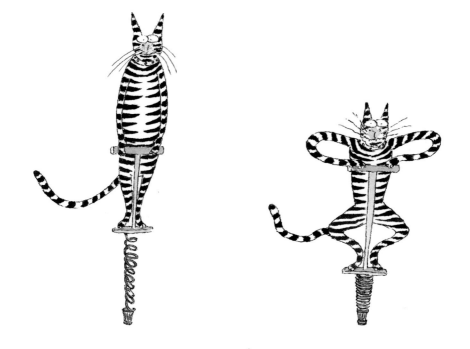

Small Pleasure no. 237, the Pogo Stick

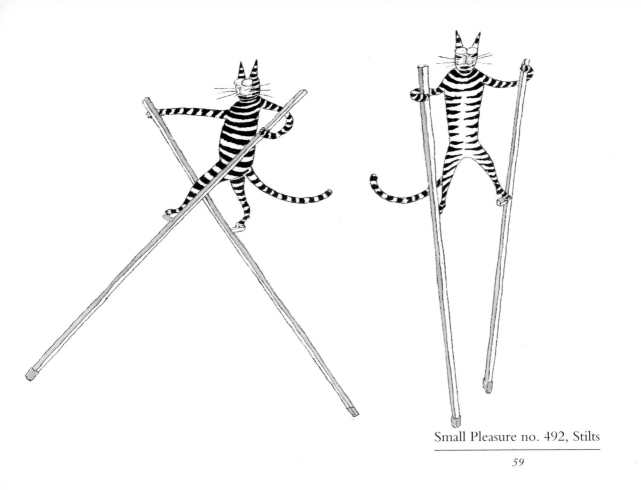

Small Pleasure no. 492, Stilts

Small Pleasure no. 35, Beekeeping

Small Pleasure no. 61, the Loom

Small Pleasure no. 49, Book-of-the-Month Club

Small Pleasure no. 119, Bagpipes

Small Pleasure no. 29, Ventriloquism

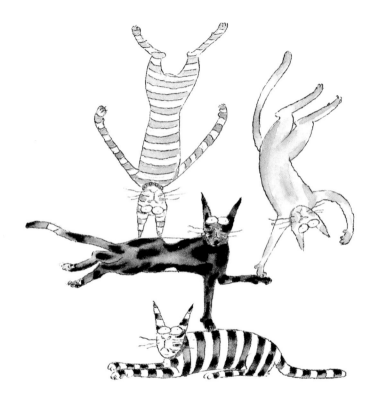

Small Pleasure no. 105, Catnap

Small Pleasure no. 2, Wool

Cats in Costume

Algeria

India

Lappland

Chile, Argentina, Uruguay

Spain

New Zealand

Beauty
Cats

Beauty Parlor

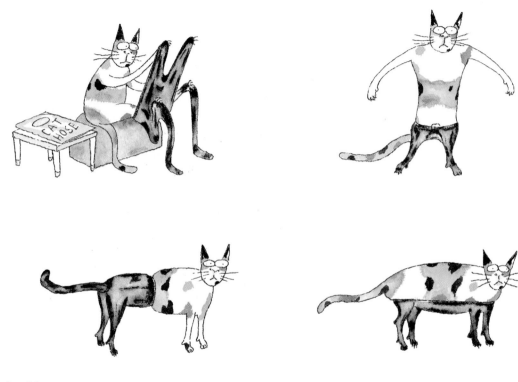

Cat Hose

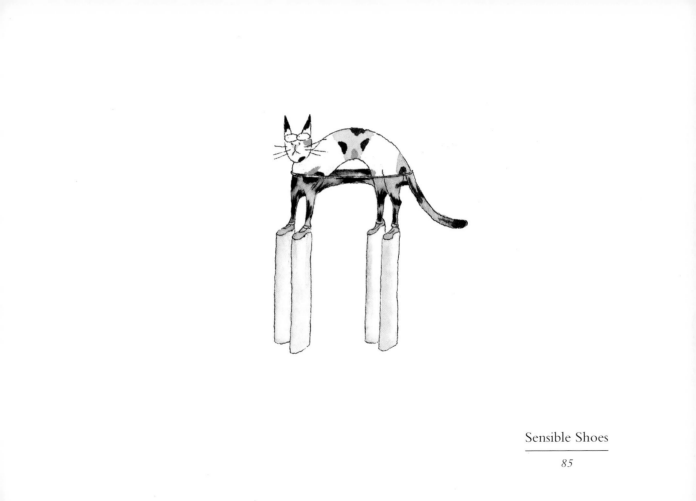

Sensible Shoes

85

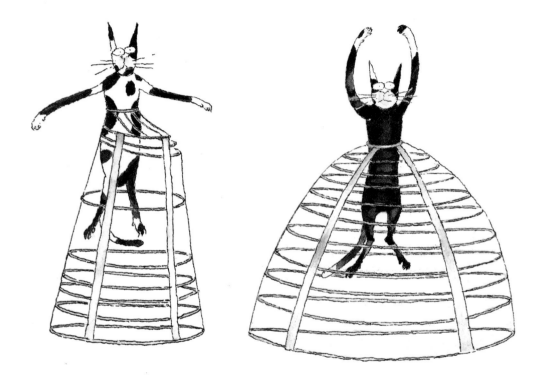

Crinolines

Corset

False Eyelashes

Cat Wax

Leek   Marigold   Sardine   Swiss   Stilton   Strawberries
and Cream

Cat Wraps

Cat Tucks I & II

95

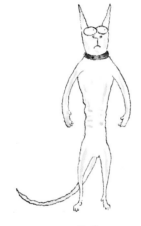

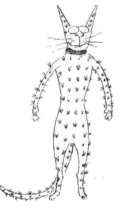

Before   After

Hair Club

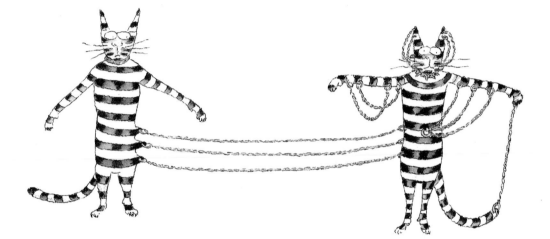

Body Piercing

Implants
_____
100

Mud Mask

Index

Index

VICTORIA ROBERTS is a cartoonist whose work appears regularly in *The New Yorker* and *The New York Times*. She has written and illustrated eleven books in England, Australia, and the United States. She lives in New York City with her husband and her pug, Pogo.